MORE PRAISE FOR "GOTCHA!"

"I thoroughly enjoyed reading about Brett's cell phone lost & found adventures, happily anticipating the next story and the next story. Brett is a great storyteller. I was amazed at his good fortune, had so much fun reading the stories and was moved as well by the generosity of so many people."
-Rebecca Suzanne Scott, Holistic Healer, N.Y.C

"A light-hearted but powerful read on a problem we all can relate to. The miracle of this book is that each situation has a delightful resolution."
-Jerry Simons, Infectious Disease Specialist, N.Y.C

"I first have to say wow, crazy turns into heartwarming! I'm an usher at AMC Theaters and find many phones while cleaning the auditoriums. I feel so happy to find their phones. I know the feeling! Expensive item!

One guy came out of a movie looking for his phone in the lobby. He looks familiar -- WHEN HE GETS CLOSER I REALIZE IT'S HUGH JACKMAN. I assist him in the phone search; he uses my iphone to call his iphone. Hugh finds his phone in the bathroom trash can! He thinks when he was texting his driver, he was throwing the paper towels away and dropped the phone (oy!)

Wow Brett, you're some author!!!!!!!!!! Made my day to read!!!! Great stories!!! Great writing!!! Love your book!"
-Phillip Schachter, AMC Usher, N.Y.C

GOTCHA!

40+ TIMES I LOST + FOUND MY PHONE HOW?

A TRUE STORY

BRETT EDELSTEIN

ISBN: 9798375044972

Book Layout designed by Drew Clark
Website: drewtolife.com

I dedicate this book 📚 to all the lovely 😊 people who as I say were beyond lovely 😇 to give me back my phone 📱. It takes having a heart 🖤 of gold to hand ✋ someone back their phone ☎️. Typically, people lose their phones 📞 and never 👎 get it back.

A NOTE TO THE READER

Throughout the book, you will notice that each lost phone event is preceded by the exclamative:

BRETT YOU LOST YOUR PHONE!

With a big smile, I tell you the inspiration, for this, is a beloved childhood book, <u>Froggy Gets Dressed</u>, in which the author, Jonathan London, uses a recurring exclamative: "Frrrooggy-Did you forget to put something on?" I just love that, so in tribute I bring my own story forward with my own exclamative, and "thanks Froggy"...

XI

XII

PREFACE

The story begins many years ago as a young boy getting his first cell phone. He is now 27 and in all this time, he has never lost a phone—or rather has never had a phone stay lost. The young boy, Brett (me!), is the luckiest boy ever, and you will see why when you read this funny, charming and heartwarming true story.

Believe it or not, the never-truly-lost-phone has been found more than 40 times by some very polite, lovely and responsible individuals from all walks of life who came to the rescue and reliably returned the phone to him.

Just as a disclaimer, while completely true, this unbelievably amazing journey through the decades does not apply to the same phone, but to all of the phones the young boy has had.

Most of the photos shown are recreations, taken at the actual location of the "lost phone," to keep to the spirit of where these incidents actually happened.

Island Sound
Wading
quebogue
ead
24
Westhampto
Beach
Shirley
27

"BRETT, YOU LOST YOUR PHONE!"

ON HAMPTON JITNEY

...ON THE HAMPTON JITNEY

My travel companion.

THE INCIDENT: I am only six or seven years old. Imagine being all alone on the Hampton Jitney Coach Bus. I have a phone practically glued to me, because I am all alone, experiencing the hustle and bustle of the Jitney. To make matters worse, my mom is a nervous wreck, as it is the first time that I AM ALONE ON THE JOURNEY. I am traveling on the Jitney to the Hamptons to visit my grandparents. My mom enlists the "bus supervisor" on board the bus to please watch over me, and made her promise she'd help me get off the Jitney at the right stop. Mom also spoke to a woman, traveling on the bus with a young child, who was sitting right behind me, and asked her to help me with anything I needed. And finally, my mom promises to call me on the cell phone I am carrying and speak to me throughout the entire trip.

Once the bus gets going, the first thing the "bus supervisor" does is inform me I cannot use the phone, my lifeline, and to put it away. She even forbids me to use it, telling me to, "Sit still and put your phone away 'til we get there." So much for watching out for me!

As I sit there, waiting for the phone to ring, I am truly madly, deeply panicking that my mom isn't calling me. Does it occur to me to wonder where my phone might be since I haven't heard it ring? Not really.

THE SAVE: Remember the lady with the child that my mom requested to watch over me? She hears the phone ringing. I probably had been sitting on the phone, which is why I didn't hear it. Once I stood to get off the bus, it fell behind the seat. As my mom had been calling incessantly, the lady heard the phone ringing and picked it up from the floor. And just in time, as I'm leaving the last bus step into my grandparent's arms, she hands me the cell phone. (For complete accuracy, my mom lent me this phone and she was using my dad's phone to keep in touch.)

"BRETT, YOU LOST YOUR PHONE!"

IN CABS

...LOST IN CABS

With diversions like this on every NYC corner, you could forget anything.

A phone can slip so easily out of your pocket when you sit down. Something I have experienced in too many taxicabs to count. Here are the most memorable instances.

THE INCIDENT: When I was younger, there was no "Find My," feature or what used to be called "Find My Phone." It's the feature that helps you find your phone when it's lost, but only if the phone's not dead. And we did not have the ability to lock the phone, so we relied on calling it whenever it went astray. God forbid, if it wasn't charged, then we would be out of luck.

Like all the other times, it was really scary when I lost my phone. This was only the second time. My mom called the phone and luckily it was charged. But she was still angry and nervous and upset—and then surprised when a young man actually answered.

THE SAVE: The phone was next to him in the cab and he picked it up and answered it. My mom told him that this was her son's phone and we really needed it back. She said she was willing to meet him wherever he was going. It was lunchtime and he was going on a BLIND DATE (You can't make this up!) at a fancy restaurant in

Gramercy Park. The guy said he would take the phone with him on his date to the restaurant. He described what he was wearing so my mom could find him and his date.

It was actually a small, intimate restaurant, which made it easy to find them. My mother said that they seemed like a well-suited couple. Hopefully, my mom and I helped the couple's romance along. My mom told the bartender to give them Prosecco flutes from us, in gratitude. I like to think they got married because of us.

...MORE CAB STORIES

THE INCIDENT: In a Taxi. As per usual, I didn't realize my phone was missing until my mom came home. She informs me that she has been trying to call me. I go to find my PHONE and it is GONE!

THE SAVE: The phone is FOUND in a cab on East 86th Street. A lovely woman picks up the phone and answers when I call. She tells me she is a doctor's assistant. She doesn't want to leave it with the cab driver, as phones are valuable. She decides to bring the phone to the doctor's office where she can lock it up. Since it's too late to meet now, she says she can meet us the next day at lunch. She refused a tip, as was usually the case with people who returned my phone. As I said, most of the people were lovely. My whole family was impressed by all these acts of kindness.

THE INCIDENT: Traveling all of Manhattan to get my phone back. It sure kept me busy. These are the incidents in cabs I remember most: #4: 34th Street in front of Macy's, which felt like a scene out of A Miracle on 34th Street, and how I had to hustle so far from where I live. #5: Cab on West 72nd Street and #6: Cab on the Lower East Side (LES).

THE SAVE: It usually went this way: The cab driver brought the phone back. Sometimes it was because we called, and sometimes they'd phone the last number called, which of course would be my mother, and sometimes, they'd recall our address and leave it with the doorman.

 SAVE #7: One time a cab driver brought the phone back from LaGuardia Airport. He had dropped me off at home and gone back to the airport when he found the phone. He remembered MY address (believe it or not). He then came back to my building and described me to the doorman. The doorman called up, and mom and I raced down to thank the driver. Despite wanting to give him a tip, HE JUST SMILED AND SHOOK HIS HEAD AND REMARKED, "I HAVE KIDS, TOO!" This happened most of the time.

14

"BRETT, YOU LOST YOUR PHONE!"
ON A TRAIN

...ON AMTRAK TRAIN

THE INCIDENT: Lost on NE Regional #173 train from New London, CT to Penn Station. Rushing to get off the train, I left the phone in the front seat pocket.

An Amtrak attendant on the train somehow noticed that I left it there. He leaves the train to follow me to hand me my phone, but he loses me in the crowd. I realized my phone was lost when I went to CALL my mom as I had promised I would when I got off the train. The dilemma: Should I meet my mom at the prearranged location of the southernmost staircase? OR, instead of meeting there, wouldn't it be more grown-up, to go directly to the LOST + FOUND? Mom would be proud, I thought, if I went to report it missing, and maybe, I would find it was there.

THE SAVE: Obviously, My mom doesn't know where I am. She's calling the phone constantly (familiar theme). Here's the part that's TRULY MAGICAL: A man answers and says he has the phone, and that your son left it on the train. It's THE ATTENDANT from the train. He's talking to my mom, but not only can she hear him on the phone, but she can see him, because he's right in front of her! She tells him, "Do you know you are in front of me?" LOL...So he gets off the escalator on the street level floor and hands her my phone. That he found my mom there is amazing -nothing short of wizardry- since Penn Station is huge and where she was standing is not the main entrance. We can only attribute this telephone find to spiritual intervention. It's that wild!!!

So now my mom has the phone, but she has no idea where I am and she really starts to panic. She decides not to budge from where she is waiting, but it's getting late. So, just as any anxious mom would do, she decides to go outside the door to get a better vantage point, while still being able to see if I came out that door. Then, 45 minutes later, she sees me sauntering nonchalantly down the sidewalk...she runs to me carrying MY phone. I was very confused. While I was trying to locate the Lost and Found (not easy at Penn Station) to report my phone missing, she was at our meeting spot and somehow the phone had showed up with her there. This is really one of the TOP true stories, perhaps my personal favorite. My mom's favorite is coming up, look for Lily's sidewalk. This one is mine.

I trekked over to Penn Station to give you an idea of how absolutely amazing it was to have the phone find me in this huge place.

"BRETT, YOU LOST YOUR PHONE!"

ON CITY BUS

...ON NYC BUS

Marvel at how NYC bus speeds away!

THE INCIDENT: Lost ON the M103 BUS at night coming back from the 92nd Street Y. I don't know how I lost it, but I realized it when I returned home. After much calling around, we find that we have to go to New York City Transit's Lost Property Unit. It's actually located in the 34th and 8th Avenue subway station, on the lower mezzanine, way underground, and it's very intimidating.

As soon as you open the door you're exposed to GLARING FLUORESCENT lights giving you an instant headache. This place felt like a police station and that I'd done something wrong. I had to wait in line and was given a form to fill out about the missing item, including its description and anything else I could remember about my phone. It wasn't enough to just say I lost my cell phone and the number. I was feeling really sad and depleted and for the first time, I thought I'd really never see my phone again. I just waited and waited and waited and then they called me up to this little open window counter.

THE SAVE: The lady handed me a little zip-top plastic bag, and there inside was my phone, totally out of juice aka no power. Phew! I had to sign for it—never did that before—and show proper ID. But once again I had my phone back in my hands.

"BRETT, YOU LOST YOUR PHONE!"
AT RESORTS

...AT SOUTH SEAS ISLAND RESORT ON CAPTIVA ISLAND, FL

THE INCIDENT: I'm laying on the pool chaise lounge. When I get up to leave, I'm in a hurry and I forget my phone. That can happen to anyone, but lucky me, it was hand-delivered back to my father before I knew it was lost.

THE SAVE: The security man in charge of the hotel's Lost + Found called our room and my dad answered. As I didn't know the phone was lost, when I got back my dad surprised me by telling me that the man in charge of the Lost + Found had my phone and we could meet him in the lobby after dinner to get it back.

Here's the backstory: You're probably wondering how they knew it was my phone. The pool attendant and I had become friendly when I was talking to him at the chaise lounge, and he knew it was my phone since we became friends on Facebook. So lovely.

Later, he told me MY PHONE GOT TANGLED UP in the towels. My family and I were all laughing about how this story exemplifies what makes me so lucky. It could have had very different endings. Obviously, the phone could have gotten wrapped up in the towels never to be seen again, lost in the washing machine or it could have been transferred to the security guard and put in the Lost + Found.

But what are the odds the guy stripping the chairs of the towels would recognize MY phone and tell the security guard to call my room? He truly, madly, deeply, particularly knew me. BTW: The phone was dead, of course.

...IN FRONT OF LILY'S BUILDING

This happens to be my mom's favorite story, you'll see why.

THE INCIDENT: Lost the phone in front of "Lily's" building on the sidewalk. The building is on Park Avenue and 94th Street. I told Lily that I lost my phone and SHE called my phone for me. She spoke to a truck driver, who had picked up my phone. He said he was bringing it back to his boss in the Bronx.

THE SAVE: I called my mother from Lily's phone and told her my phone was picked up by a deliveryman and he was bringing it back to the Bronx to his boss. At this point, it was my mother's mission to get in touch with the boss before the phone ran out of power. Here's what the boss told my mother: "The delivery man from his uniform-cleaning company found the phone on the street and brought it back to him."

My mom asked if the delivery man was going to be making any more deliveries in Manhattan, and the boss says he won't be delivering until the following Wednesday. And it was Friday.

She then asks if she can come to the Bronx to pick it up, as the weekend was coming up and her son needs the phone.
Then he says, and here's the part that's hard to believe, "Wait a minute, where do you live?" and she tells him, and he says, "We service the uniforms in that building!" Then he gets real friendly and says, "Since you live in that building, I will have my guy bring the phone directly to you tonight."

This is the other part that's always so hard to believe, then he says, "I'm a granddad and I know all about lost phones." And yes, true to his word, the driver delivered the phone later that evening and refused a tip.

12

35

...IN FRONT OF BLACK BUILDING

You can sort of see the lovely doorman

THE INCIDENT: Lost my phone on 66th Street and Second Avenue on the ground in front of The Black Building.

THE SAVE: A doorman calls, saying, "Someone gave my phone to him." By this time, my mom had glued a sticker to my phone that said, "If lost, call her number" and it worked, he called. We went to pick up the phone and I kissed it, a ritual that had become part of getting back my phone. BTW, the doorman refused a tip.

"BRETT, YOU LOST YOUR PHONE!"

ON A PLANE

38

13

39

...ON A PLANE TO VERMONT

THE INCIDENT: My mother and I took a trip to Vermont to visit a school for an interview. As soon as we get to the hotel, we GET A CALL FROM THE AIRLINE that my phone was left in the front seat-pocket.

THE SAVE: We are only there overnight. They tell us they are leaving the phone at the check-in counter at the airline and we can ask for it there. Sure enough, it was waiting there in a zip-top plastic bag with my name on it... and yes, it was dead.

41

...IN DISNEYLAND, CA

Zippidy-doo-dahing down Splash Mountain...unaware of what's to come years later!

THE INCIDENT: Now my mom decides to put my phone in a rubber straightjacket that I wear around my neck. (Actually I have several of these holders in different colors.) But somehow, I managed to lose both the phone and its holder when we were at Disneyland. It must have been when I was between rides or whatever and besides, the phone wasn't exactly on my neck...

THE SAVE: IF YOU'RE AS FAMILIAR WITH DISNEYLAND AS I AM, SINCE I'VE BEEN GOING THERE MY WHOLE LIFE, YOU KNOW THAT AS YOU ENTER, THERE ARE BATHROOMS AND THE LOST + FOUND. I realize my phone is lost when I get off of the Splash Mountain ride. It's a real trek to get back to the Lost + Found. I AM FAMILIAR WITH LOST + FOUNDS AND THIS ONE IS VERY EFFICIENT. Evidently, there are a lot of lost phones at Disneyland. I could easily identify mine because it was in a black rubber holder. I didn't even have to give my telephone number. I was handed yet another zip-top plastic bag with my phone sealed inside and of course, it was dead.

13

43

...IN RENTAL CAR LOS ANGELES, CA
[I LIKE TO CALL IT LA LA LAND, PLUS MY DAD'S SIDE OF THE FAMILY LIVES THERE]

THE INCIDENT: This time, my mom is really upset. Usually she is upset, but this time, she's frantic. She's been calling my phone nonstop and getting no answer. We just came from the Queen Mary (the ship) and she's certain I left it there. We don't have time to retrace our steps. (BTW, ON THE QUEEN MARY, I got an original tie at this Art Deco festival being held there. I still have it and love it...Okay, back to the story.) We have dinner plans with our family and it's at the kind of place you have to show up right on time with your group or you will not be seated. And we are late; so my mom is torn between finding my phone and getting to the restaurant. It's really unusual for me to have no idea where my phone is. MOM ONCE AGAIN HAS TO CALL THE LOST+ FOUND... THIS TIME SHE CALLS the Queen Mary and speaks to the Lost + Found and to my disbelief there is no phone in a plastic zip-top bag waiting for me. My mom says to me she thinks it's really lost this time, and on and on and on...until we join the rest of the family we are meeting.

44

We forget about the missing phone during dinner. After dinner, when we get back to the car, my mom remembers the missing phone and calls it incessantly. I have to hear her panic the whole ride back to the hotel.

THE SAVE: When we get back to the hotel, my mom is still calling the phone (feels like it has been for hours!). When we open the trunk, we hear a soft ringing coming from inside it. It was hard to hear, but it was like a heartbeat to me. We searched and searched until finally we found the phone underneath where the spare tire would be stored. I have no idea how that happened. Guess it slid somehow. This time it was in a different kind of holder. Made of black fake leather, it had a clip that went over the waistband of my pants. Don't ask how it got off my jeans...BUT there it was, near the spare tire. I took it out and kissed it, AND BOY, WAS I GLAD TO SEE IT! AND OF COURSE, I WAS GLAD, TOO, THAT IT HELD THE CHARGE...

45

46

16

47

...IN LOCKER AT YMCA

It never gets old...

THE INCIDENT: The YMCA on 14th Street. I went to the YMCA with my school for weekly swimming lessons as part of what they called Physical Arts. One morning, after changing in the locker room, I left my phone. And it remained there the whole day of school and into the evening. It wasn't until after I got home and my mom got home from work, THAT I REALIZED THAT THE PHONE WAS MISSING...

THE SAVE: My mom springs into action and immediately calls the Y on 14th Street. After being transferred about three times, she finally gets to the head of MAINTENANCE AND SHE IS PUT ON HOLD WHILE THEY CHECK IF THE LOCKERS HAD BEEN CLEANED. I AM WATCHING AND LISTENING IMPATIENTLY AS SHE GETS THE NEWS THAT THE LOCKERS WERE CLEANED AND THAT "NO PHONE WAS FOUND!!!" But my mother wanted to make sure for herself, just in case. So off we went to the Y, and since it was the men's lockers, she pushed me through the door into the now vacant locker room.

Luckily for me, I opened just a few lockers and came quickly to the correct one—and my phone was there! I took it to my mom waiting outside the locker room, and she and I were so happy to have rescued it! As usual, it was not charged, which as you know, makes it harder to find.

48

49

...ON TARGET'S FLOOR

Lost my phone on the floor again! Went back to document.

THE INCIDENT: I went to check out the new Target store between 69th and 70th Streets on Third Avenue with my friend, Elliot. And when I got home much later, I realized my phone was GONE. How? My mom told me she kept calling the phone and no one answered. It kept going to voicemail. She tells me to retrace my steps and find the phone.

THE SAVE: I make it back to the Target store before it closes and ask a few people if they found the phone. They direct me to security. There it is, in a zip-top plastic bag. In order to retrieve it, I had to describe the case. Evidently, the phone fell on the floor and found its way to security, yet again. AND IT WAS DEAD...

LORENZO'S CAMP
PARSON'S
ANCIENT TOWN
SOAPSTONE QUARRIES
EMERALD BAY
INDIAN ROCK
HOWLAND'S
SULLIVAN'S
SILVER GREY GOATS
ROAD
IRONBOUND
RIBBON ROCKS
BULL'S HEAD
CATALINA HARBOR
WEST POINT
MUSSEL ROCK
B
C
G
BACHELOR PT.
NORTH HARBOR
WHITE ROCK
HARBOR
YACHTS
STEAMER PIER
PLEASURE PIER
BUENA VISTA PARK

...ON BOAT TO CATALINA ISLAND, CA

My mom and I posing for the photo

THE INCIDENT: Actually this one I don't recall so well because I had thought that I left my phone in the car or back at the hotel. But my mother had reminded me that I had used it on the boat. I had to wait the entire day to approach Security at the Catalina Island Hydrofoil to find out if it was really lost.

THE SAVE: Security went into the back and came back out holding the now familiar zip-top plastic bag. Again, I had to identify my phone by both the case and the telephone number. I was relieved and kissed it, happy to be able to perform this ritual that meant my phone was back.

"BRETT, YOU LOST YOUR PHONE!"

AT A CONCERT

...AT TAYLOR SWIFT CONCERT IN MADISON SQUARE GARDEN

...had a blast seeing Taylor Swift.

THE INCIDENT: It was at a really fabulous TAYLOR SWIFT concert at Madison Square Garden. As would be predictable, I jumped up and down a lot during the concert, so my phone fell out of my pocket.

THE SAVE: This is one of the times I realized the phone was gone almost immediately but the crowd was going the reverse direction I needed to go to retrieve my phone. When I finally made my way against the crowd to get back into Madison Square Garden, the guard at the door asked to see my ticket stub before he let me in. They were already cleaning up the theater. He escorted me to my seat and he used his flashlight to look all around it for my phone. Then before my very eyes, I saw IT beneath the seat. I GAVE IT A QUICK KISS.

58

"BRETT, YOU LOST YOUR PHONE!"
ON CITY STREETS

...DROPPING CONSTANTLY ON THE FLOOR

Typical encounter for my phone...on the street.

THE INCIDENT: I can't count the number of times it has happened that my phone dropped on the sidewalk or in stores. People would bump into me sometimes, or for whatever the reason, the phone would fall. And LUCKY for me and thanks to strangers' kindness, helpful people around me would see it happen and would scream, "Excuse me!" really loud to get my attention that I had lost my phone. Believe it or not, I only actually cracked the screen on the phone once, at the Verizon Store, when I was there to get a new battery. Oops! I dropped it.

25

63

...AT THE BEACON HOTEL RESTAURANT BEFORE CONCERT

THE INCIDENT: Lost in the Beacon Hotel Restaurant right before the Mariah Carey Christmas Spectacular Concert [which by the way, I won the tickets for, but that is another story]. I realized my phone was lost because I was trying to take photos of Mariah Carey and could not find my phone once again!

THE SAVE: After the concert, we scurried back to the restaurant, which was nearby. Although the restaurant was closed, we were directed to see a man at the bar who handed me my phone in, you guessed it, a zip-top plastic bag. My phone was dead of course, as always.

64

26
to
33

...IN A MYRIAD OF RESTAURANTS

Sarah Beth's CPS the maître d' let me take the photo, and such a charming guy, told me, he could put an APP on my phone, Find My, to locate my phone. I smiled and said only if it's charged.

THE INCIDENTS: I have left my phone at many restaurants: French, Italian, Greek, Vegan, Turkish, Thai, American, and Cafes, etc. I either left it on the table or it fell underneath. I lost it at Joe Allen's (#26) in the Theatre District.

At all three locations of Sarabeth's: Upper East (#27) later found under the table by the waiter but we didn't know this since we had gone home. That time it was worth losing my phone because I got to schmooze with the "beyond lovely" maître d'. We retrieved the phone the next day.

On the way home from Sarabeth's Central Park South (#28), I realized I had lost it while on the taxi ride home. It was already put in the vault and the manager was gone so I had to return the next day. It had been put in a zip-top bag. That time, believe it or not, I lost my phone and my elephant shaped cross-shoulder bag. I call it an elephant bag because it really is an elephant shaped bag. Both items were returned at last!

Grabbed lunch with my friend Ann and got this photo just in time. Mercer Kitchen is now closed.

Sarabeth's Upper West (#29). It was found under the table once again. We were sitting way in the back and it was candle-lit so I could not possibly see my phone under the table. It was very late and I didn't know I lost it until the next day, when I called and found out it was there, of course!

THE INCIDENT #30: Lost it on the table at Tavern 29 in Rose Hill. I lost my phone and the waitress returned it.

THE SAVE: The matronly waitress screamed at me in an Irish brogue from across the whole street, "Hey you... you forgot something. Come here and get it." Not only did I forget my phone, I also forgot my wallet. [BTW, my mom did not know about me losing my wallet until we were drafting this book. Also, just a tidbit, this night at the pub was the first night I tried Crabbies ginger beer. I was with my friend Elliot again on our usual Friday night get-together.]

THE INCIDENT #31: At Mercer Kitchen, a restaurant way downtown in SoHo, trendy at the time. We were almost home in the cab, when I realized I LOST IT. So my mom and I stayed in the cab

70

and went all the way back to the restaurant, and then home again. IF you are wondering, the cab did wait while I ran in.

THE INCIDENT #32: Barbaresco on Lexington, where my family and I are regular customers. I had walked out of the restaurant but knew right away that I had lost the phone. So I went back inside and the waiter snottily handed me back my phone. He said in a low voice, "Here's your phone," which he had wrapped in a linen napkin.

THE INCIDENT #33: Orsay on Lexington. The loss took place on a Tuesday evening when I was there with my friend Vicky. We had a lovely time! I didn't realize that the phone was missing until the next day around lunchtime. I gave the restaurant a ring to ask if they had found my missing phone. The eloquent French man who answered the phone was "beyond elegant and helpful" and said they had it there. I had to verify it was mine with my telephone number. (My mom did not know this story either until the reading of the book draft.)

THE SAVE: The elegant Frenchman actually DELIVERED my phone to my doorman. His only request was that I call him to tell him that I received it. What a beyond lovely gentleman! My friends Lynette and Ashia were visiting that day, which is the reason I ASKED the lovely Frenchman to DELIVER my phone to my building. As my friends were leaving, they actually had forgotten that I had needed to get my phone in the lobby. They hadn't been with me the night before (that was my friend Vicky) and they forgot I even had to retrieve my phone in the lobby of the building... as forgetful about the phone as I was all the times when I lost it! I DID CALL THE FRENCHMAN AND TOLD HIM I GOT THE PHONE, AND THANKED HIM.

72

"BRETT, YOU LOST YOUR PHONE!"

IN STORES

34 to 35

75

...AT DRESSING ROOMS IN STORES

The next two places I lost my phone everyone can relate to. Who has not left their phone in a dressing room when it's easy to get distracted by trying on clothing? Am I right? The most memorable times were at American Eagle (#34), where the salesman, who was also the cashier, pursues me into the street, locates me, sprints up to me and says, "You left your phone in the dressing room." The other time I can remember is in the Levi's Store in SoHo (#35), but that time I realized the phone was missing just as I was leaving the dressing room and went back to get it. And I'm sure there are many more times that I can't remember.

...AT POXABOGUE DRIVING RANGE

I gently placed the phone down, at the scene of the Golf Center parking lot, to recreate the intense moment of sheer joy when I found it. Can you get the vibe?

THE INCIDENT: I was at the Golf Center; Poxaboque in Bridgehampton, New York, to practice hitting balls at the driving range, and everything was going fine. I was about to go to their luncheonette called Fairway and wanted to check my email and Facebook, when I realized my phone was GONE! I retraced my steps, first to the bathroom, then to the Pro Shop, to the place I got my drink. And then I did a thorough inspection of my golf bag and all of my pockets. It was nowhere to be seen!

THE SAVE: Then, I thought maybe the phone was in the CAR because I knew I had it when I arrived. I searched the car. NO PHONE! I was very despondent. I was going to go back to the center, opening the opposite car door and just as I was about to put my foot down and smash whatever was on the floor, THERE IT WAS! MY PHONE WAS LYING HELPLESSLY ON THE ASPHALT. I picked it up and kissed it, as was now the ritual. I breathed a sigh of relief and hugged it! My mom remembers this particularly clearly because my grandpa almost stepped on a watch in the same lot...

...AT LONG ISLAND SUMMER PROGRAM

I should have lost my phone in this corn maze instead of under my couch.

THE INCIDENT: I was spending the summer at a program in Long Island when I realized I had lost my phone. Unfortunately, at the time, I was on an outing. A small group of us had gone to the beach. I told the person in charge that I did not have my phone. A guy around my age overheard and he volunteered to help me find my phone. Since I did not have it on me, we checked both the seating at the stand overlooking the beach where we had eaten lunch as well as the van we had ridden in. IT WAS NOWHERE TO BE SEEN! I checked myself several times as well as all the places we went to. When we returned from the beach, the guy who had helped me search, whose name was Ben, decided to come to my apartment and help me look for my phone there. But we had no LUCK in finding it. He then checked some parts of the grounds where we were staying and to see if my phone was in the Lost and Found. Finally, Ben said he was sorry but he couldn't find it —and gave up.

THE SAVE: Ben lent me his phone and I called my mom, who was with friends, visiting my grandma's pool in New Jersey. She was in the locker room with her friend Linda, and out of all things to call about, I had to tell my mom that I lost my phone. And just as I was speaking to her, I found my phone underneath the pillow of the coach.
I KISSED THE PHONE AND LET OUT A SIGH OF RELIEF!

80

38 to 41

81

...AT HOME

You're probably thinking how hard is it to find a phone in your own house—very! When it is dead.

THE INCIDENT: For over three long days and nights, I had no idea where my phone was. (#38) I SEARCHED MY ROOM and every place I could think of. I retraced my steps but no phone. My mom must have called it 100 times with no answer. Obviously, it wasn't charged. I knew I needed help finding it, so I called my friend Vicky, who I call VickyAnna as a nickname. You might ask why we did not disable the phone. That was because my family and I knew the phone must be in the house. When expert phone finder VickyAnna arrives, she asks a few questions to narrow down the search. At first, she was helping to organize random things around the house, since our apartment always could use attention.

THE SAVE: VickyAnna summed up the situation, then returned to the couch and expertly unhooked the two connecting couches. My phone fell down with a thud, just as she was unhooking the couches. [BTW, our couch is called a Sofa and Chaise Sectional.] Evidently, it was caught between the two couches. I wonder if VickyAnna is a "Phone Psychic." I was laughing when all this happened, and VickyAnna said that once I have my own apartment, this really would be serious and not a laughing matter. I'd be crying if that happened! My mom agreed and we all laughed about that.

THE INCIDENT #39: Found in some random jacket pocket or pants pocket but the phone is always dead so our go-to app, Find My, never actually works. Therefore, it becomes a scavenger hunt to locate my phone.

THE INCIDENT #40: Lost in couch pillows. I must have lost it a dozen times in the pillows. Because the phone is always dead, I can't call it or use the Find My app. That is when it becomes a scavenger hunt yet again!

THE INCIDENT #41: Other favorite hiding places of my phone are under magazines, piles of clothing and mixed up in the comforter of my bed. I must have spent hundreds of hours searching for my phone in the apartment alone.

This is noteworthy -- It was a time I did not lose my phone but I lost my keys. (That is why it's a bonus story). I left my keys in my apartment during my time in the summer program in Long Island. I wound up sleeping over at my family friend Debbie's mother's house [her name is Eleanor] since I could not enter the apartment.

Here's how it happened: I had gone out to dinner with Debbie that night and it was quite an adventure in itself as we ate far away at a bar near the beach. When Debbie dropped me off, I realized I didn't have my keys. Just then, I saw the Program Supervisor, Donna, ride by in the van with the kids in my program, but I was caught off guard and didn't think to flag her down. Instead, I called Debbie from the door of my apartment and she came back to get me. Obviously I didn't have any clothes or anything packed to stay over at her mother's house. An aside, Debbie kept making fun of the fact that my mom had written a note-card on the door reminding me to check the weather, and I did not even have my keys to get in! Lucky for me, this time I had my phone to call Debbie.

I slept that night in the famous Johnny Bench room as Debbie reminds me now. (Debbie is a huge baseball fan and had filled that room with JB memorabilia.) I also got to meet Debbie's mom, who very graciously let me stay over very last minute, indeed. Debbie's right that I should have had a reminder to not leave my keys instead of just checking the weather on the note card of reminders in my apartment...

86

Duxbury
Moretown
Charlotte
Faystown
Waitsfield
Warren
Hancock
Philadelphia
Pitsford
Hubberton
Benson

"BRETT, YOU LOST YOUR PHONE!"
ON VACATION
Newbury
Topsham
Stockbridge
Waterquechee R.
Hartland
Killington
Bridgewater
Woodstock
RIVER
WINDSOR
Shrewsbury
Saltash
Reading
Sugar R.

...AT WOODLOCH RESORT

This has nothing to do with the phone- my family won "gold medal"- our proudest moment. Had to share.

THE INCIDENT: I lost my phone somewhere in the Woodloch Resort, where we used to visit during the Winter Holiday Vacation in the Poconos. I did not know I lost my phone until late at night when my mom asked if I charged my phone. My eyes bugged out because I realized my phone was...GONE! Even though it's late, my mom insists that we contact security. We got through to an old guy who answers the phone and tells us he does have the phone, but we have to come get it and ID it...the usual drill.

THE SAVE: You would think that since there are so many kids running around that place, they would be very relaxed about handing phones back, but NO! IT WAS ALL VERY SERIOUS. We were instructed to meet him outside near the North Lodge, and it was very dark and cold. He acted very cop-like, asking me a lot of questions about my phone before he returned it to me. I have NO IDEA why we were outside in the dark and not inside the warm, comfy lodge. I briefly recall he said he was on his way home, so that's probably why we met outside.

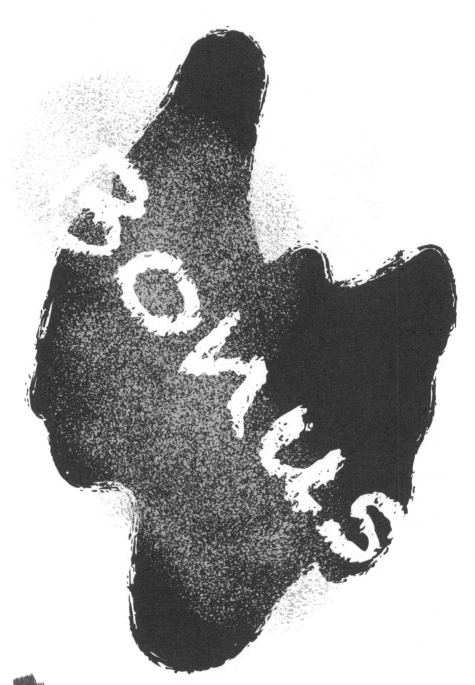

91

...UNDERWATER

Then it happened THE UNTHINKABLE...THIS VERY INCIDENT.
My family was visiting my granny apple, granny's pet name, at her
pool. It was a beautiful day and I could not wait to get in the pool.
My dad had the same idea, but he still was putting on his sunblock
while I rushed to the water. And just as I jumped in— I was still
in mid-air —when I realized my phone was in my POCKET!!!
NOOOO!!!!!!!!!!!! I told my dad and he thought I was kidding. I
fished it out and attempted to revive it. My friend, VickyAnna, gave
me instructions for how to fix my phone by putting it in rice. She's
savvy about those kinds of things! I followed this recipe and waited
and waited and waited for it to work. Finally, my mom said it wasn't
working, so it was time to get a new phone after all.

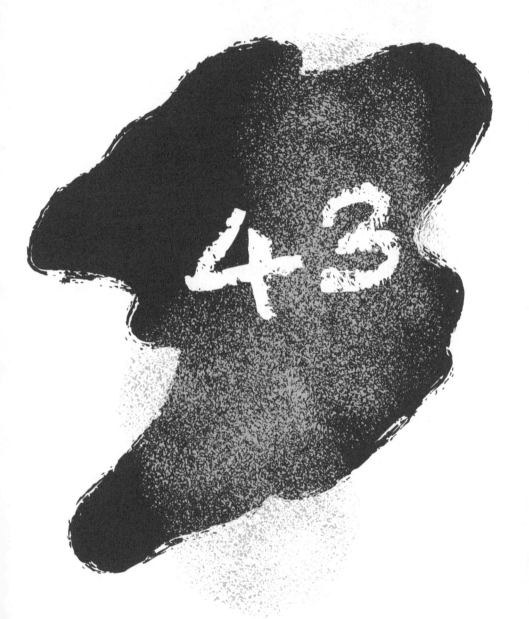

93

...IN FRONT OF BLOOMINGDALE'S

This is where I dropped my phone it's a bad place to drop it—lots of people around to grab it—in front of the subway.

So I have a brand-new phone in what is the "forest green" color with a see-through case. And it is back to its old tricks.

THE INCIDENT: I dropped it—my shiny new phone—in front of the subway station, 59th Street in front of Bloomingdale's Department Store. Of course, I didn't realize I lost it until I got home. Now this is kind of funny... my Mom attempted the FindMy app a dozen times. Nothing seemed to be working! WE STOOD THERE IN OUR APARTMENT IN A STATE OF SHOCK AND SADNESS. We couldn't believe it. My mom was getting really nervous and pacing back and forth. She was really not cool, saying, "WE MUST DISABLE THE PHONE, NOW."

My dad, however, decides as he usually would, "It hasn't been lost that long, give it one more time." So he tries calling the number one last time and a young lady answers. My dad, however, is not practiced in how to speak to someone who finds my phone; usually my mom is the one doing it. He's very MATTER OF FACT and he scares her. NOW HERE'S THE REAL FUNNY PART...we were able to track the whereabouts of the phone and saw it was very far away,

SOMEWHERE IN QUEENS. The woman who found the phone tells my father that she picked it up in front of the 59th Street subway station and decided the safest thing to do was take it home with her. She was sorry that she could not answer sooner but she had been in the subway all that time.

THE SAVE: NOW COMES THE EVEN FUNNIER PART...when my dad had asked the girl where she lives, she got nervous and kind of intimidated. So my mom grabs the phone at this point and says, "Thanks so much for finding the phone. What would be the best place to get the phone back?" The young woman tells my Mom, "Your dad wanted to pick it up tonight." My mom giggles and keeps going and says, "What would be the best way to get the phone back?" Probably feeling uncomfortable giving her address to complete strangers, the woman explains she is a dental hygienist and that she works near the 59th Street subway station. After she gave her work address, she said we could pick up the phone at noon the next day.

When my mom goes to pick it up, the dental hygienist REFUSED A FINDERS FEE and not only had she CHARGED IT but she returned it CLEAN AND FRESH AND SMELLING OF ALCOHOL in a zip-top bag!!! UNBELIEVABLE!

...AT SCHOOL IN LOCKER

I never lost it on the school bus— amazing!

THE INCIDENT: I happened to remember this story at the last minute as I was finishing this book. What happened is actually pretty amusing...I was in a taxi after school, going to my gym, located on the Upper West Side. I was not using my phone at all for most of the taxi ride but I decided to check the time to make sure I wasn't late. At which point, I realized that my phone was MIA. Linett, a friend I was traveling with, "googled" the name of my school to find the number. Thanks to cell phones and Google, she swiftly got the school on the phone and told the secretary, Crystal, what had happened. I just had a flashback in my head to this vivid memory. At the time, to have the chance to see a number retrieved on Google was very exciting! Linett was very tech-savvy, so googling the number of the school felt like it came out of the clear blue. This was a decade ago, when people had to be tech-savvy in order to retrieve telephone numbers on phones back then.

THE SAVE: Of course, I had to wait until the next day at school to retrieve my phone. But lucky for me, as with all the other incidents, my phone was waiting, all wrapped up in paper with my name on it ready for me to kiss once again. I also was very friendly with the secretary, Crystal and Amelia, the receptionist, so they were very happy to tell me they had found my phone inside my locker. I checked all the missed calls and emails and also told my mom that I got my phone back...

98

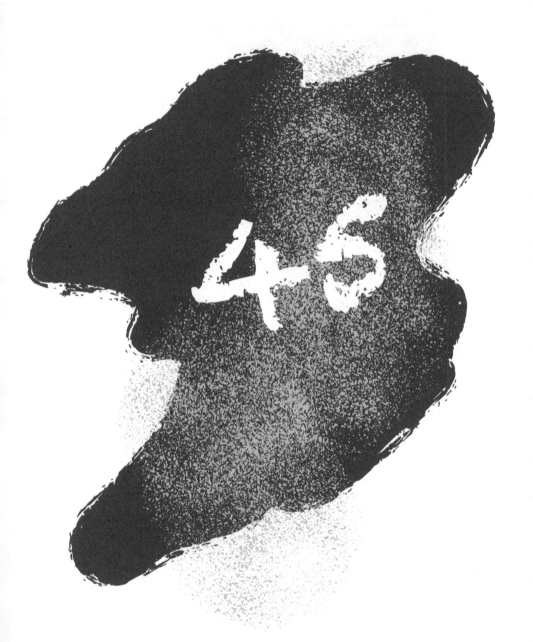

99

...AT LA PLAZA GARDEN

This is the only photo in real time, documenting the actual phone pick up as it happened—perfect timing.

THE INCIDENT: This just occurred this past weekend. We went to the La Plaza Garden as part of the 11th Annual LUNGS (Loisaida United Neighborhood Gardens Harvest Arts Festival), located in Alphabet City. And oops, I did it again! My phone drops out of my pocket/hand and this rough voice yells out to me as they're passing, "You dropped YOUR PHONE!" My mom, who is the supporting character in this very story and in life itself, insists on taking a photograph of me to commemorate the save.

This is how I feel when I find my phone.
The world loves my phone and me.

THIS IS THE END OF A LONG, LONG JOURNEY. After having lost my phone on a hydrofoil (boat), a train, bus, plane, cabs/rental car and a Jitney, as well as in restaurants, at concerts, on city streets, at resorts, the YMCA, on the beach, at the pool, retail stores, in my house, etc., I KISSED THE PHONE AND PUT IT IN MY POCKET TO START THE REST OF MY ADVENTURES.

UNTIL NEXT TIME,

YOUR FRIEND,
BRETT EDELSTEIN

Thank you very much for reading my book. Bye for now. If you'd like to share your Lost & Found phone stories, please post on my blog, **gotchaphone.com**. For general or press inquiries, contact me at **brettcedel@gmail.com**.

...ALL ABOUT ME

I attended Thames Academy at Mitchell College and then
Marymount Manhattan College. My interests include writing ✍,
working on my own jewelry line; Molton Ice 🧊, playing guitar
🎸 with my own technique, visual art 🖼, painting 🎨, ceramics and
sculpture, along with marbleizing. My most recent passion is
ice 🧊 skating.

Made in the USA
Monee, IL
22 March 2023

29719814R00070